W9-AHA-549

The Dust Bowl

Edited and introduced by
David C. King

Dust Bowl

Larger area
affected by
dust storms

Discovery Enterprises, Ltd.
Carlisle, Massachusetts

All rights reserved. No part of this book may be reproduced, stored in a retrieval system, or transmitted in any form or by any means, electronic, mechanical, photocopied, recorded, or otherwise, without prior written permission of the authors or publisher, except for brief quotes and illustrations used for review purposes.

© Discovery Enterprises, Ltd., Carlisle, MA 1997

ISBN: 978-1-57960-018-1

Library of Congress Catalog Card Number 97 - 77592

Printed in the United States of America

Subject Reference Guide:

The Dustbowl
Edited and introduced by David C. King

The Dust Bowl — U. S. History

The Great Depression — U. S. History

Photo Credits:

Cover illustration:
Farm, Cimarron County, Oklahoma, 1936, by Arthur Rothstein

Pages 4, 18, and 50 by Dorothea Lange

Page 48, courtesy of the Franklin Delano Roosevelt Library

All other photographs in this book are by Arthur Rothstein.
They were selected from *The Depression Years As Photographed by Arthur Rothstein,* Dover Publications, New York, 1978.

Table of Contents

This famous photo, **Migrant Mother, Nipomo, California,** *by Dorothea Lange, expresses the anguish felt by many in the Dust Bowl years. (Courtesy of the Resettlement Authority)*

Introduction

by
David C. King

*"This is the dust storm country. It is the saddest land
I have ever seen."*

— Reporter Ernie Pyle

*"I say, look again. You see the set of that chin. You
see the way that mother stands. You see the straight line
of that man's shoulders. You see something in those faces
that transcends misery."*

— Roy Emerson Stryker, Director,
Historical Section,
Farm Security Administration

The "Dust Bowl" was a term used to describe both a region and
a moment of history in the mid-1930s. After years of drought, a
large area of the American Great Plains was devastated by dust
storms. Millions of tons of powdery dust that had once been rich
topsoil were lifted into dense, dark clouds the people called "black
blizzards." From the Dakotas in the North to Texas in the South,
from the Mississippi River Valley in the East to the Rocky Mountains in the West, an area of 150,000 square miles became a desolate
ruin. The parched land, stripped of its topsoil, turned into a dreary
desert, incapable of supporting the homesteading families who had
settled the region.

When the first dust storms struck in November, 1933, the farm
families and townspeople were already reeling from the effects of

the worst economic depression in the nation's history. During hard times in the past, a family with a little land could at least raise enough food to see them through. But the dust storms destroyed that traditional bit of security and people found themselves with nothing. In the hardest hit areas, more than sixty percent of the people were forced off the land.

Thousands of displaced farm families became migrants. They made their way to the cities or to other agricultural regions, hoping to find some way to survive. The largest numbers went to California in the hope that there they might resurrect their American dream. The government launched a variety of programs to offer short-term relief and long-term solutions. Some of the programs helped. Some didn't. The most devastating effects of the Dust Bowl did not end until the Second World War, when the increased demand for agricultural products and the resurgence of industries created both work and hope.

Like other chapters in the story of the Great Depression, the episode known as the Dust Bowl is a deeply moving human drama. The drama may sometimes be obscured by the maze of statistics and analyses we resort to in trying to explain what happened in America during the 1930s.

Several developments, however, led to the creation of a remarkable historic record of the Dust Bowl that allows us to glimpse that vital human dimension beneath the facts and figures. One of these developments was a growing interest in gathering eyewitness accounts. Throughout the Great Depression, hundreds of journalists, government workers, and others listened, observed, and recorded episodes in the lives of people deeply affected by massive economic, social, and political forces.

Two other developments were more specific to farming and to the Dust Bowl experience. The first of these developments was the creation of what was called the "Historical Section" of the government Farm Security Administration (FSA). This unit, directed by

Roy Emerson Stryker, brought together some of the nation's best photographers. Armed with "scripts," or outlines, written by Stryker, they spent months at a time wandering the countryside to document the unfolding of history.

The photographers—Dorothea Lange, Walker Evans, Arthur Rothstein, Ben Shahn, and others—compiled an amazing record of some 270,000 photographs. They followed Stryker's direction to "look for the significant detail—the kinds of things that a scholar a hundred years from now is going to wonder about." The result was a constant stream of photographs that were reproduced in newspapers, magazines, and books. In the short-term, the pictures helped people understand why the relief efforts of Roosevelt's New Deal were so desperately needed. In the longer-range terms of how we see our past, the FSA photographs put faces on the statistics and show us our kinship with the people who lived through those dark days. This selection of eyewitness accounts and government documents of the Dust Bowl features the photographs of Arthur Rothstein.

Dust Bowl farm in Oklahoma, 1936

The second event that has produced the unique historical documentation of the Dust Bowl was John Steinbeck's novel, *The Grapes of Wrath*—the tragic and courageous story of a family driven from their farm, who become migrants seeking a new start. Steinbeck was deeply influenced by the FSA photographs. As Stryker later recalled:

Source: Roy Emerson Stryker & Nancy Wood, *In This Proud Land: America 1935-1943 As Seen in the FSA Photographs*, Boston: NY Graphic Society, 1973, p. 14.

I remember when Steinbeck came in and looked at the pictures for a couple of days. Those tragic, beautiful faces were what inspired him to write *The Grapes of Wrath*. He caught in words everything the photographers were trying to say in pictures. Dignity versus despair. Maybe I'm a fool, but I believe that dignity wins out. When it doesn't, then we as a people will become extinct.

Steinbeck's 1939 novel, and the film based on it, quickly became classics, and both book and movie have helped later generations to view the Dust Bowl story with empathy and understanding.

Farming the Great Plains: Recipe for Disaster

The dust storms, when they came, struck suddenly, beginning late in 1933. The conditions that led to those storms, however, had developed over nearly a century. It was the activity of farmers and ranchers over several decades that provided the recipe for disaster.

The Great Plains region was once a huge sea of prairie grasses. It was, and is, a dry and delicate ecosystem. Most of the region receives only 10-20 inches of rainfall each year—less than half the amount that falls east of the Mississippi and in the Pacific Northwest.

In the last half of the 19th century cattle ranchers, sheep ranchers and homesteading farm families moved in, displacing the herds of buffalo and tribes of Plains Indians that had once roamed the region. The ranchers allowed their herds to overgraze the land, denuding vast areas of deep-rooted grass that had held in the soil. The farmers, granted 160-acre sections by the Homestead Act of 1862, plowed up the thick prairie sod to plant their sprawling fields of wheat and corn. With the sod gone, the harvested fields were alternately baked dry in the sun and washed away by rain and snowfall.

For a time, the Great Plains seemed to be a Garden of Eden. Ranchers increased their herds; farmers cut down trees and plowed up the sod around their houses and barns to plant still more. Many farmers believed a strange theory that "rain follows the plow." The theory held that the plowing and planting would somehow lead to an increase in rainfall.

Hamlin Garland described the worship of wheat that gripped the Prairie farmers in the 1870s and 1880s:

Source: Quoted in David C. King, et. al., *The United States and Its People*, Menlo Park, CA: Addison Wesley Publishing Co., 1994, p. 424.

As I look back over my life on that farm, the song of the reaper fills a large place in my mind. We were all worshippers of wheat in those days. Farmers thought and talked of little else between seeding and harvest, and you will not wonder at this if you have known and bowed before such abundance as we then enjoyed....Our fields ran to the world's end.

In addition to overgrazing and overfarming, farmers used methods that encouraged erosion. More than a century before the Dust Bowl, Thomas Jefferson had written confidently that Americans knew how to use contour plowing to avoid soil runoff:

Source: A.A. Lipscomb, ed., *The Writings of Thomas Jefferson*, Washington, D.C., Definitive Edition, 1905, Vol. XVIII, p. 278.

Our country is hilly and we have been in the habit of plowing in straight rows, whether up or down hill, in oblique lines, or however they led, and our soil was all rapidly running into the rivers. We now plow horizontally following the curvature of the hills and hollows on dead level, however crooked the lines may be. Every furrow thus acts as a reservoir to receive & retain the waters, all of which go to the benefit of the plant instead of running off into stream. In a farm horizontally & deeply ploughed, scarcely an ounce of soil is now carried off from it. In point of beauty nothing can exceed that of the waving lines & rows winding along the face of the hills & valleys.

Alabama farmer stands by the eroded hillside, 1937

Prairie farmers ignored this knowledge. Instead of plowing to follow the contours of the land, they plowed in straight lines. Millions of tons of precious topsoil were washed away into lakes, rivers, and streams. By 1930, the State of Iowa alone reported a loss of "550,000 tons of good surface soil per square mile, or a total of 30 billion tons" for the state.

During World War I (1914-1918), when much of Europe was devastated by war, the demand for American agricultural products soared and so did the prices paid to farmers. The Great Plains farmers responded by borrowing money to lease or buy still more land to increase their productivity and profits. Many were now able to buy the new farm machinery, like tractors and combines, often paying little money down. During the war years, the region also enjoyed rainfall considerably higher than normal. For a short time, farm families enjoyed record profits.

When the war ended, so did the boom for prairie farmers and ranchers. While America and the world did not enter the Great Depression until after the Stock Market crash in 1929, the depression began in the 1920s for the nation's farmers. A government report, written in 1937, described what happened after the prosperous war years.

Source: Berta Asch & A.R. Magnus, "Farmers on Relief & Rehabilitation," *WPA Research Monogragh VIII,* Washington, D.C., U.S. Government Printing Office, 1937, p. 12.

Not only have some farmers been trying to grow crops on hopelessly poor soil, but others have been ruining good land by practices conducive to soil erosion or have failed to take necessary precautions to protect land subject to erosion. Warnings of soil erosion have been heard in many areas for years, but these have been ignored by farmers who were too eager for immediate results to care about the future. Other farmers could not afford the outlay necessary to prevent erosion or had such limited acreages that they had no choice but to use their land to the full, regardless of the danger of over cropping. In 1934, the National Resources Board reported that the usefulness for farming of 35 million acres had been completely destroyed, that the top soil was nearly or entirely removed from another 125 million acres, and that destruction had begun on another 100 million acres.

Excessive cropping has been especially destructive on the dry land of the Western Great Plains, where quarter sections allotted to the settlers under the homesteading laws were too small for economic use of the land. The farmers were further led astray during the World War, when they were encouraged to break more and more sod in order to meet the world demand for wheat. No provision was made against the effects of the inevitable dry years, & vast acreages of dry soil were left unprotected by grass or trees against the ravages of wind & sun.

Poverty Amid Plenty

A 1932 newspaper article used the case study of one farm family to demonstrate what happened to farmers between 1920 and 1932:

Source: Bernhard Ostrolenk, "The Farmer's Plight: A Far-Reaching Crisis," *The New York Times*, Sept. 25, 1932.

The most superficial study of the statistics reveals that while industry reached a new peak of prosperity between 1920 and 1929, the farmer met with one financial setback after another; that he was becoming poorer and poorer; that the disaster of 1920 was followed by an even greater financial catastrophe in 1930. That story can be told simply and graphically by considering the case of Ole Swanson —a case that is not unlike that of hundreds of thousands of other farmers.

By 1912, Ole, then 35 years old and a renter, had accumulated some $2,000 in cash, two teams of horses, a reasonable supply of implements, a few brood sows and some cattle. He decided to buy his deceased father's farm of 160 acres in Southern Minnesota for $20,000. He paid $2,000 in cash, gave an $8,000 second mortgage to the estate and a $10,000 first mortgage to an insurance company.

Between 1912 and 1920, because of exceptional thrift and competence, Ole was able to pay off the entire second mortgage of $8,000, besides improving his barns, adding more cattle to his herd, increasing his equipment, building a porch to his home and making other improvements, as well as buying furniture, rugs and books, and giving his children an adequate education.

But between 1920 and 1928 Ole found that his expenses, because of the industrial prosperity, were increasing. He had to pay more and more for labor and for goods. On the other hand, because of the drop in agricultural prices, his income was constantly falling. So, in those years, he

13

was unable to amortize his remaining $10,000 mortgage, and, moreover, found that his standard of living was rapidly declining. By 1925 his net income for his labor had fallen to less than $400 annually. His 18-year-old daughter, who had become employed in town as a typist, with no experience whatever and without invested capital, was earning $15 a week, or nearly $800 a year, almost twice what Ole was earning for his labor during that period.

In 1929 Ole was unable to meet a total interest of $600 and taxes of $300 and was compelled to give the insurance company, holding his mortgage, a chattel mortgage for the interest debt. In 1930 he was compelled to give an even larger chattel mortgage.

In 1931 his gross income was insufficient to meet either taxes or interest, and the insurance company, now having failed to get interest for three years, foreclosed the mortgage in the Spring of 1932. Ole, at the age of 55, was again a renter on his father's farm—the farm upon which he had been born and on which he had labored for a quarter of a century; having lost his entire equity of $10,000, he was left carrying a burdensome chattel mortgage.

Ole's career exemplifies the trend of American agriculture today. Not all the farmers have been foreclosed, but all are carrying heavy burdens. A mortgage of $10,000 on a 160-acre farm means that the farmer must pay $3.60 interest per acre. His taxes amount to about $1.90 per acre, making a total funded debt of $5.50 per acre. But with oats selling at 10 cents a bushel, the forty bushels he may be able to raise per acre, if lucky, will give him less gross return than he needs for those purposes alone. Certainly there is nothing left for out-of-pocket expenses, such as binder twine and tool repair, labor, seed and interest on the equity which he himself has in the farm....

The Impact of the Great Depression

In the early 1930s, as the nation plummeted into the depths of the Great Depression, the plight of farm families steadily worsened. They were farming dangerously-eroded soil to raise crops that were constantly declining in price. One result was that more and more farmers were forced to become tenants, paying the landowner a percentage of their crop. The following is from a report issued by President Franklin Roosevelt's Great Plains Committee:

Source: The Great Plains Committee, *The Future of the Great Plains*, 75 Congress, 1 Session, House Document No. 144, Washington, D.C.: U.S. Government Printing Office, Feb. 10, 1937.

There are perhaps 24,000 crop farms, covering a total of 15 million acres, which should no longer be plowed. Of the range lands, probably 95 percent have declined in forage value, this decline varying from 25 to 50 percent of its original value in southwestern North Dakota to from 50 to 75 percent in southwestern Nebraska and northwestern Kansas.

These physical changes unavoidably have been accompanied by social and economic changes. There has been a marked decline in the quality of living which could be achieved by a stalwart and energetic population....

There has grown up a confusing, intricate, and inefficient pattern of ownerships and tenures. Tenancy has increased steadily. In eight Great Plains states (not including

Oklahoma and Texas, where cotton growing outside the Plains area makes tenancy data nontypical), in 1935 more than 41 percent of all farmers were tenants. In the whole area, 35 percent of all the land in use was leased or rented in 1900; by 1935 the percentage had risen to 51. The burden of mortgages, debts, and taxes undoubtedly had rendered a much larger proportion of farmers owners only in name....

Tenancy has been a link in a chain of events which have led to instability of population within the region, to neglect of improvements, to low living standards, to insistence—sometimes included in the rental contract—upon a cash crop, to depletion of the soil, to destruction of the grass cover by overgrazing, and to a decline in the tangible and intangible values of community life. The nominally independent owner, harassed by his own burdens and carrying on an enterprise which is at present highly speculative, has not been able to arrest these tendencies. Depression and drought have accentuated trends long in the making. Tax delinquencies have brought about a vicious circle of higher tax rates on a diminishing tax base. The credit of the taxing units has declined as their debts have increased, and schools and other public services have suffered.

The prices farmers received for their products was so low that it often didn't pay to market them. As early as 1932, thousands of farm families had lost everything and took to the road. Some wandered aimlessly, hitchhiking from town to town in search of work. An Oklahoma resident described the situation to a Congressional hearing in 1932:

Source: Hearing before a Subcommittee of the Committee on Labor, House of Representatives, 72nd Congress, 1 Session, H.R. 206, Washington, D.C.: U.S. Government Printing Office, 1932, pp. 97-98.

...I talked to one man [who]...told me of his experience in raising sheep. He said that he had killed 3,000 sheep this fall and thrown them down the canyon, because it cost $1.10 to ship a sheep, and then he would get less than a dollar for it. He said he could not afford to feed the sheep, and he would not let them starve, so he just cut their throats and threw them down the canyon.

Wyoming sheepherder, 1938

The roads of the West and Southwest teem with hungry hitchhikers. The camp fires of the homeless are seen along every railroad track. I saw men, women, and children walking over the hard roads. Most of them were tenant farmers who had lost their all in the late slump in wheat and cotton....

In Oklahoma, Texas, Arkansas, and Louisiana I saw untold bales of cotton rotting in the fields because the cotton pickers could not keep body and soul together on 35 cents paid for picking 100 pounds. The farmers cooperatives who loaned the money to the planters to make the crops allowed the planters $5 a bale. That means 1,500 pounds of seed cotton for the picking of it, which was in the neighborhood of 35 cents a pound. A good picker can pick about 200 pounds of cotton a day, so that the 70 cents would not provide enough pork and beans to keep the picker in the field, so that there is fine staple cotton rotting down there by the hundreds and thousands of tons.

As a result of this appalling overproduction on the one side and the staggering underconsumption on the other side, 70 per cent of the farmers of Oklahoma were unable to pay the interests on their mortgages....

Tractored Out, Childress County, Texas, 1938, *Dorothea Lange*

Desperate Measures

As conditions grew worse for the farm families, some tried to fight against the massive economic forces that seemed to be overwhelming them. One method they tried was a "holiday" on farm selling—a sort of agricultural strike in which farmers joined together to keep products from reaching the market. They hoped that by refusing to sell, they could force prices up. The following is from a news magazine report in September, 1932:

Source: Wayne Gard, the *Nation*, Sept., 1932, reprinted in Milton Meltzer, ed., *Brother, Can You Spare a Dime? The Great Depression*, 1929-1933, NY: Alfred A. Knopf, 1969, pp. 124-125.

Torpedoes, tear gas, rotten eggs, brickbats, and planks used to puncture truck tires figure in this latest effort of our belt farmers to boost the prices of their products to the cost of production. Declaring a holiday on selling, thousands of farmers have been picketing the roads to "persuade" their neighbors to join in holding back produce for higher prices. The movement began quietly but soon was dramatized by the dumping of several truckloads of milk on a road outside Sioux City, Iowa. The pickets allowed milk and cream for hospitals to enter, however, and they donated 2,200 gallons of milk to the unemployed. Suddenly realizing that 90 per cent of the shipments from nearby milk-producers had been cut off, Sioux City people began frantically to order milk shipped by train from Omaha and to have the blockade run by trucks bearing armed deputy sheriffs. This local milk war soon ended in a price compromise....

A thirty-day holiday on farm selling was begun August 8 and later was extended indefinitely. Thus far, the strike has centered mainly about the Sioux City and Omaha markets, but lately it has spread into the Dakotas, Minnesota,

Wisconsin and Illinois. At the height of the Sioux City milk war, two thousand sunburned and overall-clad farmers were living in tent colonies along the nine truck highways leading to that city. Some were armed with pitchforks for use on truck tires. But except for sporadic outbreaks the picketing has been peaceful, and truck drivers not amenable to arguments have been allowed to pass on. On August 17, a crowd of 450 farmers, equipped with clubs and brickbats, tried to remove animals from stockyard pens in Sioux City and from trucks which had run the blockade, but this attempt was repulsed by deputy sheriffs and city policemen.

Skirmishes have taken place along some of the roads. At one point outside Sioux City, pickets stopped trucks by spreading across the pavement a section of threshing-machine belt studded with menacing spikes, but this weapon was later confiscated by deputy sheriffs. In other instances, roads were blocked with railroad ties, logs, boulders, or cables....

When a farm family fell too far behind on their mortgage, the bank foreclosed and held an auction to sell off the family's farm animals, machinery, and equipment. At some of the auctions, crowds of sympathetic neighbors used a quiet pressure to make sure that no one bid a realistic price for any item. Sometimes the neighbors bought the stock or equipment for a few dollars, then gave it back to the family. Other times, as in the following account by a journalist, they forced the auctioneer to sell the items back to the farmer for ridiculously low amounts:

Source: Ferner Nunh, the *Nation*, March, 1911, reprinted in Meltzer, ed., *op. cit.*, p. 129.

A raw, chilly day. The yard of the farm, churned black in a previous thaw, is frozen now in ruts and nodes.

Farm auction, Hastings, Nebraska, 1938

Where the boots of the farmers press, a little slime of water exudes, black and shiny. Through a fence the weather-bleached stalks of corn, combed and broken by the husking, stand ghostly in the pale air. There are no leaders, no haranguers, no organization. In fact, this is the first affair of the sort in the county.

There is a movement toward the barns. The auctioneer mounts a wagon. The first thing offered is a mare. It is rather strange that live stock is offered first; the usual order is machinery first. The defaulting farmer stands silent holding the mare; he is a man almost elderly, quiet, staid-appearing; and he stands embarrassed, smoothing the mane of the mare. The auctioneer goes through his regular cry. The mare is sixteen years old, sound except for a wire cut and a blue eye. What is he offered, what is he offered, what is he offered, does he hear a bid? He tries to make it sound like an ordinary sale. But the crowd stands silent, grim. At last someone speaks out. Two dollars. Two dollars!

Unheard of, unbelievable, why she's worth twenty times that!

The silence of the farmers is like a thick wall. The rigamarole of the auctioneer beats against it, and falls back in his face....The farmer holding the mare stands with his head hanging. At last, without raising his eyes, he says, "Fifteen dollars." This is a new and distressing business to him, and he is ashamed to make a bid of less than that.

"...do I hear a twenty, a twenty, a twenty? Why she's worth twice that much." The auctioneer is still going through the make-believe. He keeps it up for five more minutes. A pause, and a voice speaks out, "Sell her..." It is not loud, but there is insistence in it, like the slice of a plow, with the tractor-pull of the crowd reinforcing it. The auctioneer hesitates, gives in. The silent, waiting crowd is too much. "Sold." After that there is less make-believe. Three more horses are offered. They are knocked down to the farmer, with no other bids, for ten dollars, eight dollars, a dollar and a half. The farmer is learning. The machinery comes next. A hay rack, a wagon, two plows, a binder, rake, mower, disc-harrow, cultivator, pulverizer. A dollar, fifty cents, fifty cents, a quarter, a half a dollar. Sold to the farmer. His means of livelihood are saved to him.

"Hailed Out," "Grasshoppered Out"

In 1933, an outstanding journalist named Lorena Hickok began a remarkable journey that would carry her through 32 states between 1933 and 1935. She had been hired as a "confidential investigator" for Harry Hopkins, who headed Roosevelt's Federal Emergency Relief Administration. When she wrote the two letters excerpted below—the first to her close friend Eleanor Roosevelt, the second to Hopkins—she could not have known that the first of the devastating dust storms would strike in a matter of days. As her reports make clear, even before the dust storms, the farmers were suffering greatly from natural disasters—drought, hail storms, and grasshoppers.

Source: Letter to Eleanor Roosevelt from Dickinson, ND, Oct. 30, 1933, in Richard Lowitt and Maurine Beasley, eds., *One Third of a Nation: Lorena Hickok Reports on the Great Depression,* Urbana, IL: University of Illinois Press, 1981, p. 56.

Farmers, these, "hailed out" last summer, their crops destroyed by two hail storms that came within three weeks of each other in June and July, now applying for relief.

Most of them a few years ago were considered well-to-do. They have land—lots of land. Most of them have 640 acres or so. You think of a farmer with 640 acres of land as being rich. These fellows are "land poor." A 640-acre farm at $10 an acre—which is about what land is worth hereabouts these days—means only $6,400 worth of land. Most of them have a lot of stock, 30 or 40 head of cattle, 12 or 16 horses, some sheep and hogs. Their stock, thin and rangy, is trying to find a few mouthful of food on land so bare that the winds pick up the top soil and blow it about like sand. Their cows have gone dry for lack of food. Their hens are not laying. Much of their livestock will die this winter. And their livestock and their land are in most cases mortgaged up to the very limit. They are all way behind on their taxes, of course. Some of them five years!

After a succession of poor crops—this whole area apparently is in process of drying up and becoming a desert—these fellows had a good one last year. But wheat in North Dakota last year brought about 30 cents a bushel. It costs 77 cents a bushel to raise it.

This year they had no crop at all. I sat in with an investigator who was taking their stories. Again and again on the applications appeared the statement: "Hailed out. No crop at all." One man had sown—I believe, at that, they say "sowed" when they refer to planting of crops—140 acres of wheat, 25 acres of oats, 20 acres of rye, 30 acres of corn, and 20 acres of barley. All he harvested was a little corn. He was lucky, at that. I drove past cornfields today that had never grown up at all. There lay the immature stalks on the ground as the hail had beaten them down—half-starved cattle rooting around among them. From 800 acres of land one old German had harvested this year 150 bushels of wheat and seven bushels of rye....

Source: Lorena Hickok, Letter to Harry L. Hopkins from Bismarck, ND, Nov. 3, 1933, *op. cit.*, p. 68.

I'll try to give you an idea of what Bottineau [County] is like. It is said to be the worst county in the state. They haven't had a decent crop there in something like four years. Last summer the grasshoppers ate up just about everything.

The most urgent and immediate needs are clothing, bedding, and fuel. Those people haven't been able to buy a thing for four years.

Their houses have gone to ruins. No repairs for years. Their furniture, dishes, cooking utensils—no replacements in years. No bed linen. And quilts and blankets all gone. A year ago their clothing was in rags. This year they hardly have rags.

Always the plea is the same—for bedding and clothes.

Yesterday I visited one of the "better-off" families on relief. In what was once a house I found two small boys, about two and four years old, running about without a stitch on save some ragged overalls. No stockings or shoes. Their feet were purple with cold.

Sharecropper's wife and child, Arkansas, 1935

You could see light under the door in that house. The kitchen floor was so patched up—with pieces of tin, can covers, a wash boiler cover, old automobile license plates—that you couldn't tell what it might have looked like originally. Plaster falling off the walls. Newspapers stuffed in the cracks around the windows.

The mother of those children bare-legged, although she wore some sneakers on her feet is going to have another baby in January. IN THAT HOUSE. When she diffidently asked the investigator who was with me for assurance that a doctor would be on hand to see her through her confinement, I could hardly bear it.

The investigator asked to see her bedding. She hesitated for a moment. Then led us upstairs. One iron bedstead. A filthy, ragged mattress, some dirty pillows—her bed linen, she said, all gave out more than a year ago—and a few old rags of blankets. Incidentally I heard yesterday of women having babies on beds with only coats thrown over them....

"Black Blizzard"

The first dust storm struck the Great Plains on November 11, 1933. After three years of severe drought, the topsoil had become little more than a powdery dust. On that morning a fierce wind lifted what had once been farmland into swirling black clouds of dust. An estimated 300 million tons of soil were lifted into the air in the first of the "black blizzards." By afternoon the sun was blotted out in Chicago and a fine dust settled over everything—an estimated 4 pounds for every man, woman, and child in the city. The black clouds moved on, turning day to dusk in Albany two days later, then Boston, before depositing the last of the prairie soil in the Atlantic Ocean. The black blizzards continued through 1934, 1935, and into 1936.

Lorena Hickok was in Huron, South Dakota when the first dust storm hit. She wrote about it in a letter to Eleanor Roosevelt:

Source: Lorena Hickok, letter from Huron, SD, Nov. 11 & 12, 1933, in *One Third of a Nation*, pp. 91-92.

I thought I'd already seen about everything in the way of desolation, discomfort, and misery that could exist, right here in South Dakota. Well, it seems that I hadn't. Today's little treat was a dust storm. And I mean a dust storm!

It started to blow last night. All night the wind howled and screamed and sobbed around the windows.

When I got up, at 7:30 this morning, the sky seemed to be clear, but you couldn't see the sun! There was a queer brown haze—only right above was the sky clear. And the wind was blowing a gale. It kept on blowing, harder and harder. And the haze kept mounting in the sky. By the time we had finished breakfast and were ready to start out, about 9, the sun was only a lighter spot in the dust that filled the sky like a brown fog.

We drove only a few miles and had to turn back. It got worse and worse—rapidly. You couldn't see a foot ahead of the car by the time we got back, and we had a time getting back! It was like driving through a fog, only worse, for there was that damnable wind. It seemed as though the car would be blown right off the road any minute. When we stopped, we had to put on the emergency brake. The wind, behind us, actually moved the car. It was a truly terrifying experience. It was as though we had left the earth. We were being whirled off into space in a vast, impenetrable cloud of brown dust.

They had the street lights on when we finally groped our way back into town. They stayed on the rest of the day. By noon the sun wasn't even a light spot in the sky any more. You couldn't see it at all. It was so dark, and the dust was so thick that you couldn't see across the street. I was lying on the bed reading the paper and glanced up—the window looked black, just as it does at night. I was terrified, for a moment. It seemed like the end of the world.

It didn't stop blowing until sundown, and now the dust has begun to settle. If you look straight up, you can see some stars!...

Another report from South Dakota on the same storm:

Source: Quoted in T.H. Watkins, *The Great Depression: America in the 1930s*, Boston: Little, Brown & Company, 1993, p. 191.

By mid-morning, a gale was blowing, cold and black.

By noon it was blacker than night, because one can see through night and this was an opaque black. It was a wall of dirt one's eyes could not penetrate, but it could penetrate the eyes and ears and nose. It could penetrate to the lungs until one coughed up black. If a person was outside, he tied his handkerchief around his face, but he still coughed up black. When the wind died and the sun shone forth again, it was on a different world. There were no fields, only sand drifting into mounds and eddies that swirled in what was now but an autumn breeze.

Plow, covered by sand, Oklahoma, 1936

Six months later, on May 11, 1934, a second black blizzard struck. Many said that this one was even more devastating than the first. Reporter Katherine Glover described the day:

Source: Katherine Glover, *America Begins Again,* New York: Random House, 1939, p. 36.

May 11, 1934, although it passed with little notice, was almost as momentous in American history as April 6, 1917, when the United States entered the [First] World War. On that date a great dust storm blew across the continent from the plains of the West. Gray clouds choked the air for several hundred miles, day turned into night, and street lights were lighted in many cities. Railroad schedules were interrupted; roads were blocked; homes could not shut out the shifting sand; the soiling debris piled in stores, ruining thousands of dollars' worth of merchandise. Following in the wake of the storm, "dust pneumonia" took its toll in life.

As the dust storms continued through 1934 and 1935, the human suffering deepened. In Sheldon, Oklahoma, Caroline Boa Henderson and her husband managed to hang on through it all, but in 1935, she wrote of the heartbreak and misery:

Source: Quoted in T.H. Watkins, *The Great Depression*, pp. 188, 192.

We have rooted deeply. Each little tree or shrub that we have planted, each effort to make our home more convenient or attractive has seemed to strengthen the hope that our first home might also be our last....

[But now] our daily physical torture, confusion of mind, gradual wearing down of courage, seem to make that long continued hope look like a vanishing dream. There are days when for hours at a time we cannot see the windmill fifty feet from the kitchen door. There are days when for briefer periods one cannot distinguish the windows from the solid wall because of the solid blackness of the raging storm. Only in some Inferno-like dream could anyone visualize the terrifying lurid red light overspreading the sky....

[The] longing for rain has become almost an obsession. We dream of the faint gurgling sound of dry soil sucking in the grateful moisture...of the fresh green of sprouting wheat or barley, the reddish bronze of spring rye. But we wake to another day of wind and dust and hopes deferred....

A Kansas farm wife summed up the despair in two simple sentences:
"I could grovel on the ground sometimes. I feel so ...beaten."

Nature's Cruel Trick

An ironic twist was added to the gloomy picture in 1936 when one of the most destructive floods in history struck the states east of the Mississippi. Eastern farmers, like those in the West, had been overfarming the land for decades, toppling entire forests to clear more land for the plow. When record rains fell in 1936, there was nothing to hold back the torrents of water:

Source: Stuart Chase, *Rich Land, Poor Land*, quoted in Ralph K. Andrist, ed., *The American Heritage History of the 20's and 30's*, New York: American Heritage Publishing Co., 1970, p. 307.

In 1936 the Merrimac, Connecticut, Hudson, Delaware, Susquehanna, Potomac, Allegheny, and Ohio [Rivers] all went wild. The Potomac was up twenty-six feet at Washington and long barriers of sandbags protected government buildings. Pittsburgh was under ten to twenty feet of water and was without lights, transport, or power. The life of 70,000,000 people was paralyzed. The food supply was ruined, the steel industry at a standstill.

Flood

Source: David Lilienthal, *TVA: Democracy on the March*, New York: Alfred A. Knopf, 1944, p. 52.

...The dead land, shorn of its cover of grass and trees, was torn mercilessly by the rains, and the once lovely... earth was cut into deep gullies that widened into desolate canyons twenty and more feet deep. No one could look upon this horror as it is today without a shudder.

While Western farmers and ranchers longed for rain, 900 people in Ohio died in the floods and more than 500,000 were driven from their homes.

The Aftermath

For the farmers and ranchers of the Great Plains, the dust storms were the final, crushing blow after years of hardship. With their buildings and equipment half-buried in dust, their fields lifeless, there was nothing left. The banks and insurance companies that held the mortgages didn't want the land. But, to harvest one last crop, they had crews move in with tractors, plow up everything, and plant one cash crop to recover some of their loss.

To John Steinbeck, a bank was something inhuman—a "monster" that must be satisfied no matter what any humans wanted, including those who worked for the bank. In The Grapes of Wrath, *he described the final confrontation between the bank and the farm families:*

Source: John Steinbeck, *The Grapes of Wrath*, Copyright 1939, renewed 1967 by John Steinbeck, NY: Viking Penguin; Penguin Books, 1976, pp. 42-43.

...And at last the owner men came to the point. The tenant system won't work any more. One man on a tractor can take the place of twelve or fourteen families. Pay him a wage and take all the crop. We have to do it. We don't like to do it. But the monster's sick. Something's happened to the monster.

But you'll kill the land with the cotton.

We know. We've got to take cotton quick before the land dies. Then we'll sell the land. Lots of families in the East would like to own a piece of land.

The tenant men looked up alarmed. But what'll happen to us? How'll we eat?

You'll have to get off the land. The plows'll go through the dooryard.

And now the squatting men stood up angrily. Grampa took up the land, and he had to kill the Indians and drive them away. And Pa was born here, and he killed weeds and snakes. Then a bad year come and he had to borrow

a little money. An' we was born here. There in the door—
our children born here. And Pa had to borrow money.
The bank owned the land then, but we stayed and we
got a little bit of what we raised.

We know that—all that. It's not us, it's the bank.

A bank isn't like a man. Or an owner with fifty thousand acres, he isn't like a man either. That's the monster....

Yes, but the bank is only made of men.

No, you're wrong there—quite wrong there. The bank
is something else than men. It happens that every man
in a bank hates what the bank does, and yet the bank
does it. The bank is something more than men, I tell you.
It's the monster. Men made it, but they can't control it.

Dust Bowl Humor

The scene described by Steinbeck was repeated thousands of times from Montana and the Dakotas in the North to New Mexico, Oklahoma, and Texas in the South. An estimated 2.5 million people were displaced in the Great Plains states in the mid-1930s.

Even as they packed up their few meager belongings for an uncertain future on the road, the farm families had not lost their sense of humor. One Kansas farmer, for example, joked about "settin' on my porch and watching the neighbors' farms blow by." Two other examples of Dust Bowl humor:

Source: James D. Horan, *The Desperate Years*, NY: Bonanza Books, 1962, p. 165.

I'll plow next week. I reckon the farm'll blow back from Okla. by then.

Well, we haven't lost everything. The wind blew the whole damn ranch out of state, but we ain't lost everything—we still have the mortgage.

Some displaced families found temporary relief in shelters set up by towns, counties, and relief organizations like the Red Cross. In exchange for work on roads and similar projects, people received meals and a place to sleep, at least for a few days. The monotony of the meals led one anonymous participant to write one of the most popular songs of the Depression years. Written in 1932, the song became one of the hymns of homeless workers and farm families—no doubt you've heard Bacon, Beans and Gravy. *(See Janet Beyer and JoAnne B. Weisman, eds.,* The Great Depression: A Nation in Distress, *from the* Perspectives on History Series, *Carlisl⌐ MA 1995, p. 33.)*

The Okies: Troubled Search for the Promised Land

By 1935, more than half the farm families in the hardest-hit areas had been hailed-out, grasshoppered-out, dusted-out, and finally tractored-out by the banks. Cesar Chavez, who later gained fame as a union organizer for farm workers, recalled the feeling of insecurity that came with losing the family farm:

Source: Studs Turkel, *Hard Times: An Oral History of the Great Depression*, New York: Random House, 1970, pp. 53-54.

Oh, I remember having to move out of our house. ...One morning a giant tractor came in, like we had never seen before. My daddy used to do all his work with horses, so this huge tractor came in and began to knock down his corral, this small corral where my father kept his horses. We didn't understand why. In the matter of a week, the whole face of the land was changed....

We all of us climbed into an old Chevy my dad had. And then we were in California, and migratory workers....It must have been around '36. I was about eight. Well, it was a strange life. We had been poor, but we knew every night there was a bed there, and that this was our room. It was sort of a settled life, and we had chickens and hogs, eggs, and all those things. But that all of a sudden changed. When you're small, you can't figure these things out.

On the Road

With nowhere to turn, the families took to the road. Those who had vehicles—beat-up Chevys, Ford Model Ts, rusted LaSalles—piled their belongings on roofs, running boards, and bumpers.

Migrant to Oregon, from South Dakota, 1936

Every car and truck sagged under the weight of its load—pots and pans, rolled up mattresses, chairs, jugs and pails, farm tools, all wound 'round with yards of rope. Families without vehicles dragged their goods on wagons, wheelbarrows, and makeshift carts.

Some families headed to the cities and large towns, where some were lucky enough to have relatives to put them up. Others tried neighboring farm regions, hoping to find any kind of work, usually without success. By far the greatest number went West. They crowded onto US 30 through the hills of Idaho into Washington and Oregon, and in larger numbers, they jammed onto Route 66 through New Mexico and Arizona to California—the promised land.

In the last half of the decade, an estimated 300,000 of these migrants streamed into California. No matter where they came from, they were called "Okies." One member of this throng was Woody Guthrie, who later became one of the nation's best-known composers of folk songs. Guthrie said about his start as an Okie:

Source: Quoted in *Annals of America,* Chicago: Encyclopaedia Britannica, 1985, Vol. 15, p. 452.

...don't know nothin' about music. Never could read or write it. But somehow or other, when the black dust hit our country, I was among the first to blow. When it cleared off again, I woke up with a guitar in one hand and a road map in the other one.

Pete Seeger, another singer of the Great Depression era, sings at the American Youth Conference, 1940.

One of the most popular songs Guthrie wrote was "So Long (It's Been Good to know Yuh)" which became a favorite ballad of the Dust Bowl years. The song, which had many verses, began:

Source: Edith Fowke & Joe Glazer, eds., *Songs of Work and Freedom,* New York: Folkways Music Publishers, Inc., 1950 and 1951.

So Long (It's Been Good To Know Yuh)

I've sung this song, but I'll sing it again,
Of the people I've met, and the places I've seen,
Of some of the troubles that bothered my mind,
And a lot of good people that I've left behind. So it's

So long, it's been good to know yuh,
So long, it's been good to know yuh,
So long, it's been good to know yuh,
What a long time since I've been home,
And I got to be drifting along.

I walked down the street to the grocery store,
It was crowded with people both rich and both poor,
I asked the man how his butter was sold,
He said, one pound of butter for two pounds of gold; I said:

So long, etc.

Young Tramps

Some of the dispossessed wandered aimlessly, especially individuals without families. Thomas Minehan wrote about the plight of teenage boys and girls who became tramps. In the following excerpt he describes the difficulty of obtaining clothing:

Source: Thomas Minehan, *Boy and Girl Tramps of America*, New York: Farrar & Rinehart, 1934, pp. 82-83.

It was in December and very cold. Snow covered the ground. The thermometer had touched zero more than once the preceding night and morning saw its continued descent.

Dressed as a transient, registered and living at the missions, eating and sleeping with the men and boys, working for my soup and bed, taking the compulsory shower and fumigation, I attempted to obtain needed clothing. Without an overcoat beyond a well-worn blazer, buttonless and out at one elbow, with a pair of trousers out at the knee and in the seat, with an old summer cap that had hung for years in a furnace room, with worn tennis shoes covered by patched rubbers, with a pair of unmatched canvas gloves, I attempted to get some clothes through the regular relief agencies all to no avail.

My journey started in a reefer [boxcar] where Boris and I huddled together with three older men transients in the front of the car, the animal heat of our bodies making an ineffectual effort to keep us warm. We have been riding only two hours, but it has been a long cold two hours, and no swaddling of newspapers can keep us warm. Boris wears a sawed-off sheepskin over two old coats, three shirts and two pairs of patched trousers. I wear a long old sheepskin over a collection of rags.

"Today might be a good day to hit the stem for some clothing," he suggests as we leave the yards and make for a mission. "It's cold and people sometimes give you clothes when it's cold. I need shoes."

And he does. But so do I. My feet are covered with four pairs of heavy socks under tennis shoes and old rubbers patched with adhesive tape. A layer of oiled Manila paper between the top two pairs of socks, keeps my feet warm enough, but the tennis shoes and rubbers look cold as an Arctic night.

We leave our sheepskins at the mission and in ten below weather solicit every agency in the city. The missions, the Clothing Center, the Travelers' Aid, the Salvation Army, the Y.M.C.A., and a dozen other smaller agencies are visited with no success. It seems to make little difference what story Boris and I tell them. The answer is invariably No. No clothes for bums. No clothes for boy tramps.

"But we gotta leave in the morning," objects Boris to the thin young college graduate behind the desk in the Clothing Center. "Lots of folks can't stand the cold in a box car and especially me. I'll freeze tonight without a coat. Don't you think so?"

No, the young man does not think so. If it remains below zero we can most likely stay another day or two at the mission. No, we cannot work for clothing. There are more calls from local cases than can be filled. We are bums and we must be on our way....

John Steinbeck described the steady movement of people toward California:

Source: *op.cit.*, p. 299.

...And then the dispossessed were drawn west—from

Kansas, Oklahoma, Texas, New Mexico; from Nevada and Arkansas families, tribes, dusted out, tractored out. Carloads, caravans, homeless and hungry; twenty thousand and fifty thousand and a hundred thousand and two hundred thousand. They streamed over the mountains, hungry and restless—restless as ants, scurrying to find work to do—to lift, to push, to pull, to pick, to cut—anything, any burden to bear, for food. The kids are hungry. We got no place to live. Like ants scurrying for work, for food, and most of all for land....

Migrant Workers in the Promised Land

The Okies quickly found that they were not welcome in California. To the people of the state, these penniless newcomers looked—and were—dirty, their tattered clothes covered with the dust of travel and roadside camps. Their faces wore a haunted, hungry expression that frightened people. Los Angeles even tried to keep them out with "bum blockades" manned by armed deputies, until the courts told them it was illegal to turn back the newcomers.

While some Okies moved to the cities, most headed for the farm fields, where huge agricultural corporations grew cash crops that required seasonal pickers. Most migrant families lived in miserable conditions. They cooked over campfires, drew water from polluted irrigation ditches, and slept under any scraps of shelter they could construct. One government inspector told of finding forty-one people living in a two-room cabin.

When word spread that a farm owner needed pickers, thousands showed up where only hundreds were needed. The owners soon found that, no matter how low the wages they offered, some would take the job.

Steinbeck described the competition for work:

Source: Steinbeck, *op. cit.*, p. 364.

...When there was work for a man, ten men fought for it—fought with a low wage. If that fella'll work for thirty cents, I'll work for twenty-five.

If he'll take twenty-five, I'll do it for twenty.

No, me, I'm hungry. I'll work for fifteen. I'll work for food. The kids. You ought to see them. Little boils, like, comin' out, an' they can't run aroun'. Give'em some windfall fruit, an' they bloated up. Me. I'll work for a little piece of meat.

And this was good, for wages went down and prices stayed up. The great owners were glad and they sent out more handbills to bring more people in. And wages went down and prices stayed up....

A year in the life of a typical migrant went like this:

Source: John N. Webb, research report quoted in Milton Meltzer, ed., *op. cit.*, p. 140.

July-October 1932. Picked figs at Fresno, Calif., and vicinity. Wages, 10 cents a box, average 50-pound box. Picked about 15 boxes a day to earn $1.50; about $40 a month.

October-December 1932. Cut Malaga and muscat (table and wine) grapes near Fresno. Wages, 25 cents an hour. Average 6-hour day, earning $1.50; about $40 a month.

December 1932. Left for Imperial Valley, Calif.

February 1933. Picked peas, Imperial Valley. Wages, 1 cent a pound. Average 125 pounds a day. Earned $30 for season. Also worked as wagon-man in lettuce field on contract. Contract price, 5 cents a crate repack out of packing house; not field pack. This work paid 60 cents to $1 a day. On account of weather, was fortunate to break even at finish of season. Was paying 50 cents a day room and board.

March-April 1933. Left for Chicago. Stayed a couple of weeks. Returned to California two months later.

May 1933. Odd-jobs on lawns, radios, and victrolas at Fresno. Also worked as porter and handy man.

June 1933. Returned to picking figs near Fresno. Wages, 10 cents a box. Averaged $1.50 a day, and earned $50 in two months.

Reporter John L. Spivak described conditions in one of the migrant camps, where people lived in what were supposed to be outhouses.

Source: Quoted in Milton Melzer, ed., *op. cit.*, pp. 141-142.

Just take the main highway from Fresno, Calif., to Mendota which is about thirty miles away and turn west at Mendota for about four miles. You can't miss it because you'll see a big sign "Land of Milk and Honey." When you've passed this sign you'll see against the horizon a cluster of houses and when you come to the sign "Hotchkiss Ranch—Cotton Pickers Wanted" turn up the side road a few hundred yards beyond the comfortable farm house with its barns and cotton shelters. There's a row of fifteen outhouses along the road....

There are two more outhouses a little way from these and those are the ones actually used for outhouses. You can tell that by the odor and the swarms of tics that hover around these two especially. This is a typical migratory workers' camp, only some have five outhouses for the workers and some have thirty. It depends upon the size of the farm....

In this outhouse where a baby girl has scarlet fever you'll find an iron bedstead. That's where the baby sleeps, the one that's tossing around in fever while the mother tries to shoo the flies away. That's the only bed and it's one of the five in the whole camp, so you can't miss it. The other six in this family sleep on the floor huddled together; father, mother, two grown brothers, a little brother, and the fifteen-year-old girl. They sleep like most everyone else in the camp: on the floor.

That barrel and rusty milk can in the corner of the room where everybody sleeps on the floor holds the water they bring from Mendota to cool the child's fever. It is four miles to Mendota and four miles back and eight miles costs a little for gas so they have to be very sparing with the water. That's why they all look so dirty—it's not because they don't like to wash. It's because it costs too much to get water—water needed for cooking and drinking. You can't waste water just washing yourself when it costs so much to get. After all, when you make thirty-five cents for a full day's work and spend some of that for gas to get water it leaves you that much less for food....

For the victims of the Dust Bowl—as for all those who suffered during the Great Depression—one of the overriding emotions was one of bewilderment. What had happened to the American dream, which had once seemed so attainable? How could there be so much hunger and misery in the land of plenty? What had become of the rewards for those who worked hard and lived decently? And how could people maintain a sense of community, or of neighbor helping neighbor, when it seemed that everyone was down and out?

The depression brought America to a crossroads. A society based on a belief in "rugged individualism" had broken down. For the first time in our history, people came to the realization that only the national government had the resources to provide some relief. President Franklin Roosevelt, and the men and women who formed his New Deal administration, were among the first to see that massive government action was needed. In simple terms, Roosevelt stated what amounted to a major shift in American thinking: "If private...endeavor fails to provide work for willing hands and relief for the unfortunate, those suffering through no fault of their own have a right to call upon the government for aid." The New Deal was an effort to respond to that call.

The Government's Search for Solutions

by
David C. King

When Roosevelt took the oath of office as president in March, 1933, he did not have a specific set of plans for addressing the massive, complex problems of the Great Depression. He promised a "New Deal for all Americans," but he was not sure what that would consist of. Harry L. Hopkins, one of FDR's closest advisors, may have summed up the New Deal philosophy best when he said, "I am for experimenting, trying out schemes which are supported by reasonable people and see if they work. If they do not work, the world will not come to an end."

And experiment they did, launching a dizzying array of programs with two goals in mind: first, to relieve as much human suffering as possible, as rapidly as possible; second, to try to correct some of the underlying conditions that had led to that suffering.

One of the first New Deal programs—the Civilian Conservation Corps—was typical of the effort to work toward both goals. The CCC, launched during FDR's first month in office, was designed to provide immediate relief to unemployed young men. Nearly half a million of the recruits lived in military-style barracks and worked at fighting fires, building roads, campgrounds, and picnic areas, and installing 65,000 miles of telephone wire in government parks and forest reserves.

The program's "soil soldiers" also planted 1.3 billion trees—more than all the trees planted in the nation up to that time. The long-term result was a major step toward ending the tremendous soil erosion that had caused so much damage.

Roosevelt was so pleased with the tree planting that he proposed the construction of a "shelter belt" of trees to protect against a future Dust Bowl on the Great Plains. Critics scoffed at the idea of foresting a stretch of land 100 miles wide and 1,000 miles long, reaching from the Dakotas through Oklahoma. The governor of Oklahoma said it would be "like trying to grow hair on a bald head." But the president pressed on with his idea, employing both the Forest Service and the Works Progress Administration (WPA). The project produced a shelter belt of 200,000,000 trees, one of the New Deal's great successes.

WPA workers repair a flood-damaged street in Louisville, Kentucky. (Courtesy of the Franklin D. Roosevelt Library)

The New Dealers' efforts to ease the plight of the Great Plains farm families ranged from emergency relief to idealistic schemes for resettling dusted out families on better land. One of the most ambitious emergency programs was the Federal Emergency Relief Administration (FERA). Headed by Harry Hopkins, the agency began by providing direct financial aid and food through the states, counties, and towns. No one, however, including Hopkins and FDR, liked the idea of direct government handouts, so FERA was quickly transformed into the Civil Works Administration (CWA). By early 1934, nearly 4 million people were at work on some 400,000 separate projects, such as building roads, schools, hospitals, airports, and anything else Hopkins could think of.

While most CWA projects involved city workers, other aspects of FERA were aimed at improving conditions for Dust Bowl farm families. In 1934 and 1935, for example, the government purchased ruined farmland and tried to restore it by means of more scientific farming methods. Although decades of overfarming made the project only partially successful, it gave the farm families hope and demonstrated that the government was trying to help.

Rural protests, like this one in Kern County, California, were
captured by FSA photograhers. (Dorothea Lange)

Developing an Agriculture Policy

Roosevelt was convinced that the government also had to take bold steps to ease the economic uncertainties of farming. In a speech to Congress, he said:

Source: Franklin D. Roosevelt, quoted in Marshall B. Davison. *Life in America,* Boston: Houghton Mifflin, Vol. I, p. 465.

The agricultural ladder, on which an energetic young man might ascend from hired hand to tenant to independent owner, is no longer serving its purpose....The agricultural ladder...has become a treadmill....When fully half the total farm population of the United States no longer can feel secure, when millions of people have lost their roots in the soil, action to provide security is imperative....

In one of the most ambitious attempts at government planning, the Agricultural Adjustment Administration (AAA) was launched in 1933 with the goal of trying to stabilize farm prices so that in good years, overproduction would not lead to a ruinous drop in prices. Farmers were now going to be paid to plow under up to half their crops of wheat, cotton, corn, tobacco, and other cash crops. This would create an artificial scarcity that would drive up the prices farmers received for the products they did send to market.

Critics of the New Deal were outraged at the idea of destroying crops and then paying farmers not to plant as much as they had the year before. But although the program had numerous flaws it did lead to a near doubling of farm income over the next two years.

In the following reading, the Director of the AAA, Chester Davis, tried to explain the benefits of the government's radical new approach:

Source: Chester C. Davis, "Toward Planned Harvests," *Review of Reviews and World's Work*, Dec., 1936.

Fifteen million acres less cotton next year, 8 million acres taken out of wheat, 10 million or more acres no longer given over to surplus cornland: these figures begin to mount up. Add minor displacements of tobacco and rice acreage already agreed upon, the figure exceeds 33 million acres, more than the entire cultivated area of Japan proper, taken out of key crops—and turned to other uses.

To what other uses? That is a pressing question nowadays, not only here in Washington but on every farm in the land. You cannot move one piece on the vast agricultural checkerboard without altering in the end the entire design. One move compels another.

The land taken out of cotton, wheat, corn, and tobacco is being fallowed and rested, or sown, speaking generally, to noncompetitive, soil-building crops. That generally means grass. The dairymen are inclined to resist the tendency (mistakenly, I believe, as dairy cows are preeminently efficient in transforming grass into proteins); but the tendency of our present programs seems increasingly back in the direction we came from far too hastily—back to grass.

There are many reasons for this. The land needs a rest. The people who have overworked it need rest also. Women and children of the farm family especially have been driven often far too hard without reward. Grassland culture is less laborious, and life upon grasslands is pleasanter than life in a skinned, high-pressure farming area, as a rule. Land in grass does not wash away. But the most immediate and pressing cause of retreat from high-pressure farming toward a more pastoral, yet modern, economy is this: It takes three or four times as much land to feed a cow on grass as it does to grow grain and feed high-pressure feed mixtures. Livestock on grass, with supplemental rations, will not produce as much of meat or milk as livestock pressed into high production by grain feeding. But we have too much milk and meat as it is; and food produced on a grassland economy over wider areas is much more cheaply produced.

The open country is not only a place to grow things; it is a place to live; and much land pleasant to live upon is unfit to farm. As we put our lands in order from the standpoint of economical production, we shall gradually accomplish also a reordering of all America as a place to live. Not only crops will move; people will move; and we shall see, I think, a widespread intermingling of those ways of life we now think of separately as rural and urban....

And in the next reading, Secretary of Agriculture Henry A. Wallace answered critics who were horrified that the AAA had authorized the slaughter of six million baby pigs to keep them off the market.

Source: Henrey A. Wallace, transcript of the *National Home and Farm Hour*, NBC, Nov. 12, 1935, Library of Congress.

PEOPLE ARE STILL INTERESTED in the 6 million pigs that were killed in September of 1933. In letters I have received following these radio talks, the pigs are mentioned more often than any one thing, except potatoes. One letter says:

It just makes me sick all over when I think how the government has killed millions and millions of little pigs, and how that has raised pork prices until today. We poor people cannot even look at a piece of bacon.

It is common belief that pork is high today because the little pigs were killed in 1933. As a matter of fact, there is more pork now and the price is lower because these pigs were killed two years ago. Let me tell the story:

For eighteen months before August 1933, farmers had been selling hogs for an average of $3.42 a hundred weight. Such a price was ruinous to farmers. The average hog grower suffered from low hog prices during this period one thousand times more than the average consumer has suffered from high hog prices during the past few months. Hog prices in August of 1933 were intolerably low, and the northwestern Corn Belt was suffering from drought. There was every reason to expect prices to continue low cause there had been an increase in the spring pig crop, and because market, which formerly had absorbed the product of as many as 12 million hogs from this country, had largely disappeared because of tariffs and quotas.

So 6 million little pigs were killed September of 1933. They were turned into 100 million pounds of pork. That pork was distributed for relief. It went to feed the hungry. Some very small pigs could not be handled as meat by the packers. These were turned into grease and tankage for fertilizer. I suppose it is a marvelous tribute to the humanitarian instincts of the American that they sympathize more with little pigs which are killed than with full-grown hogs. Some people may object to killing pigs at any age. Perhaps they think farmers should run a sort of old-folks home for hogs and keep them around indefinitely as barnyard pets. This is a splendid attitude, but it happens that we have to think about farmers as well as hogs. And above all we must think about consumers and try to get a uniform supply of pork from year to year at a price which is fair to farmer and consumer alike....

Another program designed to provide greater security to farm families was the Emergency Farm Mortgage Act, passed by Congress the same day as the AAA. The new law put a stop to bank foreclosures and empowered the government to refinance thousands of mortgages, giving the families lower interest and a longer period for paying off the debt.

The Second New Deal

After Roosevelt's re-election in 1936, the administration launched several new programs to aid the Dust Bowl region along with other agricultural areas. The Supreme Court had declared the AAA unconstitutional, so FDR pushed through Congress a new measure, called the Soil Conservation and Domestic Allotment Act. The program gave benefits to farm families who agreed to participate in soil conservation through such measures as using soil-conserving plants like clover and planting trees. The farm family, in turn, received a certain amount for each acre taken out of production for the soil conservation efforts.

A second program, the Rural Electrification Administration (REA), represented an ambitious effort to bring electricity to all rural areas. At the time, only about 11 percent of the nation's farms had electricity, and the utility companies were in no hurry to incur the expense of installing wires to remote areas with few customers. The administration made complicated arrangements with the companies to do the work and, by 1941, 35 percent of all farms were wired. REA continued to work throughout the next decade and, by 1950, 90 percent of the farms had electrical power— one of the most enduring successes of the New Deal.

In 1937, the Bankhead-Jones Farm Tenant Act established the Farm Security Administration (FSA). The agency loaned money to thousands of tenant farm families who wanted to buy their own farms. The FSA also tried to improve living conditions for the thousands of Okies who had become migrant farm workers. In California alone, some 30,000 families were soon living in clean FSA camps which the migrants themselves managed.

Finally, in 1938, a new Agricultural Adjustment Administration was established. Through a complex system, the government once again attempted to control the wide swing in prices paid to farmers. When a surplus was produced in any given year, the government purchased the surplus, stored it, then released it during lean years when prices otherwise would have skyrocketed.

The Bahains, FSA clients from Colorado, 1939

The second AAA, like other New Deal efforts, was far from perfect. Critics maintained that farmers were being helped at the expense of consumers and taxpayers. The farm families themselves were frequently irritated by government interference and by the tremendous increase in bureaucratic red tape.

When the United States entered World War II in December, 1941, however, most of the criticism melted away. The New Deal had managed to keep most of the nation's farm population in operation and had enabled Great Plains farm families to correct some of their most serious difficulties. As a result, American farms were able to produce the huge amounts of agricultural products needed during the war years, with enough left over to feed millions of people in a war-ravaged world.

Suggested Further Reading

Beyer, Janet and JoAnne B. Weisman, eds. *The Great Depression: A Nation in Distress.* Carlisle, MA: Discovery Enterprises, Ltd., 1995.

Hunt, Irene. *No Promises in the Wind.* New York: Berkly Publishing Co., 1970.

Lowitt, Richard & Maurine Beasley, eds. *One Third of a Nation. Lorena Hickok Reports on the Great Depression.* Urbana, IL: University of Illinois Press, 1981.

Melzer, Milton, ed. *Brother, Can You Spare a Dime? The Great Depression, 1929 - 1933.* New York: Alfred A. Knopf, 1969.

Steinbeck, John. *The Grapes of Wrath.* New York: Viking Penguin, 1939, 1976.

Terkel, Studs. *Hard Times: An Oral History of the Great Depression.* New York: Random House, 1970.

Watkins, T.H. *The Great Depression: America in the 1930s.* Boston: Little, Brown & Co., 1993.

About the Editor

David C. King compiled the readings for this volume and wrote the portions that are not firsthand accounts. He has written more than thirty books for young people, primarily in American history, including *Thomas Alva Edison: The King of Inventors*, *The Age of Technology: 19th Century American Inventors*, and *First Facts About American Heroes* which was selected by the Children's Book Council as a Notable Book for 1997. He and his wife Sharon Flitterman-King live in Hillsdale, New York.

Other titles in this *Perspectives on History Series* include:

To order a catalog or book from
Discovery Enterprises, Ltd. call 1-800-729-1720.